I0435437

THE KING…and other TALES

Political Satire in the Style of
Seuss, Poe and More

by
G. P. Smith

Edited by
J. Morris

ISBN: 1523808896
ISBN-13: 978-1523808892

The King

CONTENTS

The King

.

1—DUB-YA

The man once known simply as Dub-ya,
Did really believe he was truly blessed;
He thought he could do many wonderful things,
But what a storm would rage, who could have guessed?

Not one term, but two, and neither was Super;
He still believed he could straight ahead Forge;
But as things bogged down and fell off the Rails,
Increasingly he began to resemble Curious George!

He and Teddy Kennedy hatched "No Child Left Behind,"
We were told it was great, and would lift up the Nation.
But of course such lofty delusions always go Awry,
And *this* dorky turkey nearly ruined Public Education!

9/11 occurred, and any other future choices went "Poof!"
People were stunned, then furious, demanding counter-attack;
So apparently without looking at what else might be done,
Dub-ya called for massive build-up, to go "Back to Iraq!"

Vicious, raging, bloody, deadly – and that was just the Media!
What first appeared a victory, quite easily won,
Turned out to be Illusion, and dissolved into confusion;
Shadows lifted quickly – and total guerilla warfare had begun.

Explosions, attacks, repeatedly, went on, and on, and on;
Dub-ya told everyone, "We must stay the course!"
But nothing seemed better, things were not looking good,
And Dub-ya was increasingly viewed as the back end of a horse.

Then came the Economic Crunch, which the Left had carefully crafted;
It spread Fear and Panic everywhere, as had been framed;
As planned, it struck late in the Election year,
And it was Screamed that Dub-ya should be blamed.

So Dub-ya had another fling at doing something Good;
Hoping to jump-start things, he foolishly bailed out each Crook;
Of course, they used our dough to restore their huge bonuses;
Taxpayers got screwed, the bailed-out self-indulged, and we got Took!

The last straw snapped, and the Media shredded what might have remained
Of anything and everything Dub-ya may have done right or swell;
They berated and blasted him until most were glad
He was out, and had hopefully gone to Hell!

2—THE KING

There once was a being with a mysterious past
Who wanted to rule over the land as King;
And he schemed and plotted and planned his assault
Willing to pledge, promise, bribe and say Anything.

"I can rouse them with words, do nothing good at all,
And always receive a terrific reception;
For I am most charming, glib and slippery -
A true Grand Champion of Deception."

"I will paint them beautiful, fanciful Dreams
And they will say 'We must believe his story,
For this is the one who will lead us like no other,
To Splendor, and Plenty, to Paradise and Glory.' "

He said, "If you want to have Faith and Belief,
Don't look for something you've never seen in the sky;
For the very best Provider of everything you need
Is right here before you – it is I!"

"Those who oppose us will feel the wrath
Of oppressive, life-destroying Retaliation;
We'll use lies, false facts and nasty gossip
To inflict pain, shame and Humiliation."

"I am great, I am grand,
And I am extremely clever;
If anyone doubts my magnificence,
I'll remind them - I'm the best EVER !"

"Many demand to know who I really am,
Where I've been, what I've done, and even eaten;
They shall learn to back off, stop even asking,
Or by my vicious pet Media they'll be badly beaten."

So the usual accomplices, hacks and new zealots
Burst forth in droves and mobs in a starry-eyed run,
And after the inflated polling, praise and many sorts of tricks
It was no surprise at all – they had WON!

The cheers! The tears! The screaming and ovations! All smiles,
The new King strutted forth – this was his hour!
Now he could bask in the glow of acclaim
As he began to grasp and seize total Power.

The King told his Lackeys, Hatchet People and Thugs
"The laws mean whatever I alone say;
I will crush, rip up, or completely ignore
Anything or anyone who will not OBEY!"

"I rule over this, I rule over that,
I rule over whatever else I say;
I will not stand for any complaints
For in all matters I'll have my own way!"

"Of course, what we want is completely Communist,
But everyone only teaches what we tell them to say,
People will not be allowed to know what we're doing,
Not now, not tomorrow, not next year – NO WAY!"

"Look, I'm a sinister, shadowy, arrogant King
And my wife is a self-centered cow;
But millions of people will simply believe
Whatever we say anyhow."

He took over this, he gave away that, helping his Chosen Few,
As billions became trillions, people grew scared about so much
        money;
"Never fear," said the King, "I am making great strides
Transforming this into the Land of Milk and Honey."

"I will promise them Health Care, for everyone,
And suckering them in will seal their Fate;
We'll slip in thousands of other demands, too,
But they'll never know about those until it's too late."

"Understand it, they can't, nor fix, change or run it;
It's too gigantic to know, apply or tame.
It will gobble up everything and everyone,
And absolute control will be praised in MY name!"

"They ask, 'Is this true? Is it good? Is it right?
Does it work? And is it on the level?'
But by the time they find out, it won't matter at all -
That's part of my deal with the Devil!"

At last came the day of the Almighty Roll-out,
Tens of millions were drooling and quite aflutter;
Expectations were raging, joy was barely restrained,
Then everything started to thunk, and clunk, to fizzle and to sputter.

The Collapse made folks gasp, and stare in gaping shock;
But they were told, "No, no, no, don't even worry,
Our fantastic team will use magical powers
And make it work like we said, in a huge hurry."

Months went by. The Roll-out only twitched, flickered and flopped;
But the King's ministers said, "It's not actually so bad,
As soon as we adjust and spend hundreds more millions,
It will be the Wonder we said, and you'll be very glad!"

The King proclaimed, "We can't let them think it was better before,
Truth is an Illusion, one I intend to entirely destroy;
We must keep them moving in the ways I have chosen,
For I regard every person as merely a useable toy."

Then a voice – just one tiny voice – openly said,
"Excuse me, but I'd like to speak thoughts of my own.
It seems that things have gone a whole lot worse
Since we were fooled into giving YOU the throne."

"Costs have soared, hopes have not,
Where is all the promised Employment?
For with little to do and no good job paying them
People have doubts and fears, not enjoyment."

"How is crushing Debt good, and having less Better?
And there is no end of Confusion in sight;
You say less is more, endless failures are fine,
But how can broken and useless be Right?"

Silence reigned; people were stunned, some even numb;
"No!" blurted the King, "let things just move along;
You'll see they will untangle and flow,
Because I say it, and you KNOW, I am NEVER wrong!"

Someone yelled, "You said you would improve and lift up us young
Not ignore us until we are old and wrinkled,
But as we look around and see what you've done,
We now believe on us all.....you have tinkled."

Slowly at first, with just a mere glimmer,
Folks began to shake off the foggy darkness of night;
Little by little, awareness and good sense returned,
Until they could see things as they are in the Light.

"This is not what you promised, not what you claimed,
Not what you made us believe and see;
So much is spiraling down in dismal ways,
We would rather again choose for ourselves, and be truly FREE!"

So what is next? Where will we go?
What will happen, and what will it mean?
Today what we have is horribly rotten -
What we DO about it remains to be seen.

3—THE CRAVEN

As I pondered on a weekend, bleary, while my future looked quite dreary,
    Over countless baffling rules that had appeared,
I struggled to make sense of gibberish, written by some nebish, there came
    a tapping,
    Quick and hard, a kind of rapping at the door.

Rising slowly, in confusion, I wondered what strange intrusion
    Could be interrupting my melancholy chore.
When I peered through the slats, both left and right, I could see nobody,
there in the night,
    But there came more tapping, at the door.

Slowly, with apprehension, I slightly opened the door, feeling the tension
    Of not knowing who was wanting in, or what for?
On the step I spied a motion, from a tiny apparition, and heard, "May I
    come in?
    I'm being chased by those who mean me grave volition, and I can
    run no more."

I stood there, thinking and fearing, this could go quite badly for me,
    doubting, nervous,
Wishing it would fly, vanish, or by some means go away!
But this interruption might not slam down on me, or cause more
    Intrepidation
    If just a short time he would stay.

Still feeling leery, I pushed the door out slightly, and in a heartbeat he
    hopped inside,
Rushing further into the room, very sprightly.
I closed the door and locked it securely. Turning, I gazed at the stranger,
    wide-eyed.
    Then some memory struck me, alarming me surely!

"YOU!" I cried, jabbing my finger his way, recognition hit me as if I had
    been struck
In the head by a large tuber;
For I had allowed in, to stay for however long, with no intention of offering
    aid,
    The infamous, traitorous Craven, known as Gruber!

Crossing to the cluttered table, I picked up some of my papers, and waved
    Them toward his smug face.
"YOU did this to us, saying Health Care would be great! Instead your
    schemes
Have been a total disgrace! What defense can you offer?" I cried.
    Said the Gruber, "We lied!"

"And what of those poor trusting fools you've saddled with thousands of
    rules
That have nothing at all to do with any Medical mod?"
"You've shoved them in like poison pills – do you admit that is wrong and
    odd?"
    Said the Gruber, "We used Fraud!"

"But you promised and promised no harm would be done, and only Good
    would evolve!
"Yet I wade through this mess and fail to find a single thing it will solve!"
"With such a load of needless regulation, do you want to show me how to
    save my store?"
    Said the Gruber, "We lied more!"

So whenever you are dealing with the Craven,
Do not even bother trying to find the Truth;
You might as well open a turtle's mouth
Searching for a valuable Tooth!

4—DONORS

There are people known as the Big Money Bunch, commonly known as
    "Donors:;
But truthfully they should really be labeled as what they are – the Owners.
Each side claims the *other* responds to nothing more than a cough;
Yet both grovel to them, and dip into opposite sides of the trough!

Yes they are Gepettos, together pulling unknown numbers of strings;
From State Houses to DC, they know what barrels of money brings!
They know how everyone ticks, and how to plant the seeds
That will give them the gratification of their lofty wants and needs.

Cross them even once, and Retaliation will abound!
Didn't know you had a mistress? Several will be "found."
The same for gambling, drink, drugs even stuff that is worse -
To make you suffer in every way, they will "prove" you are *perverse*!

You must understand politics is like a grocery store -
Every seat, office and space, has been bought and paid for.
Look at the Purists, who through muck and mire wade
To challenge "the System," - briefly they are known, then they "fade."

The Super Rich control everything, and will *not* let it go;
They have the operatives who make sure all things will flow;
Reducing their control is an absolute and total *must*;
There is not a single one of them we common folk can Trust!

5—WE'RE THE BEST

A Jackass was sitting on a park bench one day,
When feeling his own importance, he began to bray -
"We're the best, there is absolutely no doubt about it;
We've given away more to most, and should shout about it!"

"When folks want more, and care not about Cost,
We always deliver: at Give-aways we're never Lost!
The more they take, the more they want, and we Show
How and why it is WE are the ones they truly Owe!"

An Elephant, approaching, said "What you claim is Absurd!
Anyone who believes *that* is good, is a whiner, loser or Nerd!
Opportunity's there, so improve yourself all you Can;
Success is open for Anyone, *any* Woman or Man.'

Giving it away only makes it worse, for there's no Guarantee
The means will always be there, to make too much Free!
When you reward idleness instead of Good Work,
You make Takers look smart, and a hard worker a Jerk!

Jackass said, "Well *our* way is what more people Heed;
They're tired of working and still being in Need.
They want more of that sweet fruit for Themselves,
And we're happy to be their Santa and the Elves!"

The big E turned red. "You include frauds, slackers and the Shifty,
But no one there has Common Sense, is efficient, or Thrifty.
All you do is spend, spend, spend, every single day,
Yet you never ONCE devised a means to make it Pay!

Then you blame *us* for refusing to spend even More
But you took *trillions*, and down holes it did Pour!
What can you point to, so we can see what you Did
With those traincar loads of money you simply Hid?

Jackass brayed, "Well you've done plenty of Scamming
On policies, taxes and results, so while you're Damning
Us, get your *own* house in much improved Order;
You're the ones who first caused problems at the Border!

A common working guy came by, and simply shook his head;
He wiped his hands, cleared his throat, and firmly said:
"The blame you give each other could not be clearer,
Because you could both be screaming into a mirror!

"I don't actually care whatever you say
Because it won't be what you *do* anyway!
About Common Folks you don't give two hoots;
You may look like blonds, but you have very dark roots."

"Hear me People, for this I believe!"
And always that is how you begin to deceive.
The mental paths you make for them to get
What they want, are traps you have set."

"You think the schemes and plots you devise
Cause people to think you are smart, even wise.
But it it perfectly clear to *most* of us
You serve yourselves, and we go under the bus!"

"And now I will take leave of you,
Because I have actual, real work to do!"
So he got into his truck and drove away,
Leaving them both too shocked to trumpet or bray.

6—DC LOBBY

We are the DC Lobby who tries to look extremely good;
We always say we are for jobs, and growth, as we should.
But if you look deeply into our scheming, fickle, lusting core
You'll discover we're simply for sale, like any working whore!

We want *you* to work cheap, but that's not *our* selling offers;
Less for you, and much more for us, that is what fills our coffers!
"A fair day's pay for a fair day's work" - that is just oh, so dead;
Part time, no perks, pushed for more each day – that's here instead.

Look at the people, far, far, away, who make things over in Malay;
They work hard, show up on time, produce well, for fifty-cents a day!
Yes, they are children, but not lazy or spoiled, and useful in every way;
Instead of being warehoused in Public School, where they learn nothing anyway.

Cheap, cheap, cheap - the only way we want to pay now;
Cheap, cheap, cheap - we don't care about your know-how;
Cheap, cheap, cheap - we have *bribed* to get the best;
Cheap, cheap, cheap – from countries who pass our test!

You want a job? Fine! First be a "valuable" (slave) Intern, see,
That $100,00 degree gets you the chance to work – for free!
And if you truly believe excellent work will get you hired,
Look around – always more grads enter, and you'll be bluntly fired.

So we Lobby people are terrific at what we sell to those we own;
And they spout to everyone how we are making things *great*!
Bought-off surveys and paid-for studies always show us winning;
So we are – in a gigantic frenzy of making billions from what is cut-rate!

7—CHAMBER OF COMMERCE

There are members of the Chamber of Commerce, who once we thought
    were good;
They believed in Middle America – where we did what we knew we should;
But now they shun their Granddad's values, and core beliefs.
They want everything for themselves, no matter *our* losses and griefs!

They want cheap labor, and will sell out our country, to get their fare;
Let the Burglars in to have our jobs, and their families *swim* in Welfare;
Because the Chamber will collect on rent, purchases and more.
No matter what *we* want vast money into Chamber pockets will pour!

"Traditional American Values," the Chamber could not care less;
All they chase are dollars, more property and enormously more largess'
Greedy fools they are, and that is how they will stay -
As the foreigners *pour* in, and take our country away!

If they foolishly think they will be allowed to keep what they have earned
Then they are simply among those who have not yet otherwise learned
That the Left intends to strip all of us of everything we hold dear,
And replace it with total and complete bureaucracy run by Fear!!

8—CRUSH CHRISTIANS

Some Commie atheists looked at a steeple
And said "We must break those people!"
Watching true believers celebrate
They actually seethed with anger and hate.

The Christians must fall,
The old and the small.
They must all bend to what *we* say
'Cuz we want *nobody* to stand in our way!

About us they make a terrible fuss
And believe in something *greater* than us;
That must be stomped out, harshly not sweetly
So they surrender to our power completely.

What they believe is totally wrong
Since it frees them from our Siren's Song;
We must smash and mold them to our New Order
And force them to stop griping about our Border.

Those they don't like or accept, they must serve
For we will not let them have the means or nerve
To oppose our mighty Upheaval of values of old.
Those must be wrecked, 'til they are dead and cold!

Personal Freedom and doing what is Right?
Oh no no no, not any day or even night;
We will force them to change all their minds
If we must beat their heads and kick their behinds.

We will make life so harsh they will crumble,
Not even daring to complain or grumble;
Or we will make sure they can't pay for rent or food-
Look, we *said* you need us totally, dude!

Not taxing churches? A stupid notion;
Taxing is a powerful potion-
We take all we can and collect a reward;
Let's see if they get *that* from their "lord"!

Beaten to their knees, see if they pray
Or wise up, and do what *we* say!
Left with nothing, they'll see what is new,
And we will have shown *them* Who's Who!

9—THE PUPPET MASTER

All the Evil for all millenia that has come before
Combined cannot begin to equal the vileness at his core;
He has stolen what he needed to bully, bribe and control
Equipment, companies, resources and people, and still he demands more!

His Hatred is pure, his aim true, he destroys whoever stands in his way;
He has no use for humans, unless he can force them to advance his wiles.
He will cripple, disgrace, frighten or crush any to bend them to his sway;
It bothers him not, for long ago he fed conscience and morals to crocodiles.

He cares not who he has killed, maimed or completely ruined
As he pursues his maniacal, grasping, mind-warping Quest;
People tremble and cower whenever he makes them some sort of "offer"
Directed from his mysterious, protected Satanic Nest.

PM will scare, bribe or simply take over with Fear
Officials of all kinds – high and low – in a flash;
They have choices: some cash, more life, perhaps some hope
If they serve him well: if not, for them it will be the Trash.

Have troubles with a State? Buy Board Members they can't override;
Then slip in your Leftist policies and rules after all.
If it comes to light, nobody can trace it to him -
Let the Voters make the Elected take the Fall!

Employing his tentacles and suckers, PM has extended his clutching Fist
Like floodwaters, his Evil spreading out world-wide where he has Infested;
Secret success has emboldened him to warp and wrap even more
Into the Black Hole of Domination, where he has heavily Invested.

PM has smashed economies, chosen leaders and their rabid Storm
	Troopers;
He can destroy cities, cripple States, and the focus is on him never!
His goal is simple: one economy, one government, first for the West, then
	the Earth;
All individuals enslaved, Freedom gone, Elitist Manipulation lasting
	Forever!

He is a soul-less barbaric pagan, and absolute power his one true god;
To own or master everyone and all things is more than a mere Obsession;
For him it is the Pinnacle of Time, what will place him above all Mortals;
None before or after will have grabbed the Earth as a personal Possession!

Will he succeed or fail? Will we face destruction or a new Salvation Day?
We do not know. But all Tyrants of ages past have become Dust, and
	blown away.

10—CLINTONS

Way back in the counting of Time, Bill and Hillary met;
It did not take long for them to plot all they wanted to get.
Boil out all the minor stuff, and it comes down to Power and Wealth.
But they believed they should be careful, using much Stealth.

So they sold out completely to the Power Brokers in his Home State,
And by kissing the right rings, themselves they began to elevate.
Then they decided to *really* lift their prestige and Station -
So they totally sold out to *bigger* Crooks, and grabbed control of the Nation.

When Bill ran, they showed a Fantasy Flick, "The Man From Hope."
Of course they never showed him as a Sexual Predator who liked dope.
They *had* to change his persona, and raise up his Stock;
If they had shown the Truth, it could have been "The Crock From Little
     Rock."

In history's most biased Media coverage, they were protected for eight
     years;
Their Evil was suppressed, their Fraud hidden – they all came to cover their
     rears.
And Billy and Hilly made a Hellish pact to carry through -
They would come back, so *she* could dominate, demand, and rule, too.

On a taxpayer-paid visit, she claimed her name came from Everest climber
     Hillary,
But the truth is, he did not get to the top with Tensing until June of year
     1953;
She was pulled out into the world *long* before that,
Proving once again she has her LYING APP down pat!

But when they wanted her time to arrive, the Powerful Ones altered her
    luck;
They selected an unknown, more sellable, more moldable, more Evil
    Schmuck!
So Hillary did much to "enhance" her so-called "service list;"
All of it strategically engineered, so the facts most people *missed*!

Now they believe this is her time to *shine* and hold Sway,
But she really has much bad baggage brought along the way.

Hillary says she fell, in a way we don't know, and harshly hit her head;
So she had to put her Riding Broom away, and spend much time in bed.

She told the world her head was severely hurt when she fell,
Her concussion was so traumatic, for help, she even called the NFL.
Since her severe injury, she can't remember things she should know well,
So she's brain damaged, incontinent, and the Truth she simply *cannot* tell!

She has said, "I will bring down the One Percent,"
Ignoring her *5 mansions — she* doesn't pay *rent*!
Her Donors and Owners made the Evil Duo rich,
And except for Clinton Vengence, they will control the Witch.

Hillary's recorded lies, just *listed*, are at least four feet long;
Yet she still insists she – of course – is never wrong!
Her lust for Total Power is her absolute and driving Quest,
And has been proven many times before, her Evil will do the rest!

Hillary *never* reveals what she truly believes, her actual internal View -
Not wanting to anger Leftists, she hasn't mentioned her son-in-law is a Jew!

Hillary will grasp Power while delivering Revenge
On absolutely *everyone* she wants to stomp and Avenge;
Shakedown Bill won't even *ask* for cash, he will demand it,
Which will pretty much make him the world's most famous Bandit!

So Shakedown Bill has hit the campaign trail,
Still believing his image and BS will prevail.
He's counting on the young to believe all of his made-up tales,
Hoping they'll never know about his *wanton abuse* of countless females!

The Leftist Media says Bill would be "First Gentleman," they guess.
First Gentleman? NEVER! "First Predator and Panderer?" Oh yes!
Does any of this *bother* the Evil Duo, even a for a brief, tiny little bit?
No. Neither has a conscience, ethics or morals, so they don't give a ….chit.

If there was a slight chance of losing or having won,
If needed, Hillary would drive over a puppy and pistol-whip a Nun.
Then she would claim neither was her fault at *all*,
Because *neither* Clinton will admit blame, or take the *fall*.

If you still believe she is not totally, absolutely Vile,
Keep in mind she has her *real* Daddy - Satan – on Speed Dial!
We need to tell the *both* of them the "how" and "when" -
We will NOT put up with your venomous *crap* again!

11—OTHER CANDIDATES

These are candidates maybe backed by a well-funded Super Pac
Who want this group to knock out others by vicious attack;
How many years, hours and dollars have they already spent
Trying to get more popular than a meager *5 Percent?*

If the messages were blazing, just what people wanted,
They would have grown in strength, rather than remain stunted;
If they are seeking a "surge" from others failing,
They are most likely in for an old- fashioned flailing!

It *does* prove something people should absolutely note:
There really are those who will spend "whatever" to buy the Vote.
Make X shiny and sparkly, wrapped with ribbons and bows,
But please (Oh PLEASE!) don't ask *why* X was *chose!*

Packaging, promotions and Super – hype can Wow;
That's how we got the worthless Schmuck we have now!

12—VLADAMIR: THE RETURN
OF THE BEAR

Vlad was a highly placed Destroyer, long ago,
His duty was to extract submission, or inflict woe.
People obeyed orders, remaining under Soviet sway,
Or they were simply picked up, and forever went away.
For Vlad, when he stares out with his hellish gaze
Those are considered "The Good Old Days."

Harsh and rigid, yes; kind or forgiving, Never!
Brutality is a useful tool, in the hands of the Clever.
Fear begets Fear, if you employ it just right,
So people blindly accept and obey, day or night.

To have his beloved Soviet Union be reborn,
He is willing to crush Europe, blowing his War Horn;
Then he can begin to slake his megalomaniac thirst,
As *his* "Union" will be far larger than the first!

Absorbing all, slapping them in fetters, of course,
Like Alexander, parading as a god on his horse;
Dealing with them he will be sparing of breath -
Completely accept our Rule, or receive Death!

The decades of seething over lost power are gone;
Plotting and planning will restore a new Union dawn.
His allies are secure, all lines carefully drawn;
Now comes the Time of Conquest, capturing pawn after pawn.

His Master Strokes were to export a massive infusion
Including people, on cue, to cause horrific confusion;
While the deceived Fools grapple with returning Order,
Vlad will ruthlessly advance, border after border.

The besieged and battered, begging a cease to grief,
Will desperately accept his promise of rapid relief.
Deprived of any meaningful, decent defense,
What they built up so carefully will become Past Tense.

And the outbreak of violence will be world-wide
So there is no method of stemming the vicious tide;
It is planned for collapse to be total and complete,
And all target countries are at their destroyers' feet.

Where, facing all of this, are Western leaders' minds?
Many see what has happened, and figure, "Up their behinds!"
Invasion is conquest, no matter what the source;
And never pushing back against it? A truly foolish course!

It ruined many Empires, our enemies know that's true;
So they think we're too dumb to act, 'til there's nothing we can do.
The solution lies in a fact that really is bizarre-
We're not running our future – our enemies are!

Safe and secure, we certainly are *not;* all is ready for the first shout
So chaos can explode – water, food, power, they want us to be without;
For us to believe they will not attack, but to better judgment yield
Is the blind leading the blind through an endless mine field.

Wake up and shake up everyone you can, and *please* make them see
That surrounding us is mortal danger and treachery, our New Reality;
Time is not our friend; we are not prepared, our defenses are too thin;
Without strong action – NOW – Vlad and other foes will surely win.

13—NANCY

Nancy ran the House, as first female Speaker,
So she believes she is still a mighty VIP;
What a perfectly prejudiced Gorgon she was
The Public was never, ever once allowed to see.

Faze her, it didn't, as she snow-plowed other's views;
Criticism just made her lob bombs and launch rockets,
Nothing could slow her deliberate, driven, relentless pursuits;
Nor stop her from pouring hundreds of millions into her family's pockets!

One night she sat alone, replaying the harm she had willingly done;
A foul smell arose, a blast of smoke, and now the room held two!
The other was shrouded in black, with blazing coals where eyes should be;
Though due to her Party she had often been with fiends, what should she
    do?

The Specter spoke in a flat, icy voice, "This night will be historic!
For everything you thought you knew, has not been what it seemed.
You are being called forth because you are loyal and deserving;
The special place that awaits you is one of which you have only dreamed!"

Moving his hands, something shone. "This is the Gate. The Gate of Fate,
"And now the time has come to drop your labors, and for you to go in."
"One side leads to Glory, and all the splendor you could want;
"So choose your entry – one blesses your Goodness, the other punishes
    Sin."

This was not the sort of late-night forceful dealing she knew so well;
Even Nancy was uneasy of the dark, the sounds, and the putrid scent;
As always, seeking a way to avoid being blamed, she wondered if this was
    real?
Could the Specter truly be Guardian in charge of deciding where she went?

Finally she said, "I'm an important person, and I really *insist*
"That I be allowed to see where this actually leads!
"I simply refuse to just blindly follow some unknown path,
"For where *I* go, the place must meet all of my important needs!"

No matter her choice, either way would take her to the same ending place,
But why miss the magnificent chance to see surprise and shock on her face?
The Specter gave a curious smile, his blazing eyes aimed at her for a minute.
Then his chilling voice flatly said, "You have to pass it to see what's in it!"

14—KING 2

In the Spite House, drunk with vanity, the King was basking in success;
With massive treachery and illegal acts, they had seized absolute, Total
    Power!
Those foolish enough to snipe at him were blasted by the bought,
    accomplice Media,
And oh! How great it felt, to be ruling from an untouchable Tower!

If they had known, back then, about all of the
Devious, nasty, illicit acts that they know *now*,
He would have never been allowed again on the throne,
Not by any means, shape, form, no way, no how!

The King smiled slyly: that's how they had planned it all along.
More and better jobs? Nope! Safety and hope for good change? Never!
Take away, give away, make them suffer, tremble and howl;
If you want to be tickled by life, go find yourself a feather!

Strutting around, he raised his clenched fists; "Nobody can stop me now!"
This second term had been smooth – razing the old, and shackling them to
    the new;
Beliefs smashed, crumbled morals, altered values, no more legal hurdles -
Everyone pushed to *comply*, to be bossed around by the Elite Few!

When it would be done, with resistance gone, and terror causing consent,
He and his partners would rule the West – Vlad could swallow the East;
Their New World Order would be unlike anything before -
Once they willfully, gladly, *finally* had killed the hated Freedom Beast!

15—HARRY & OTHERS

HARRY

Moldy old Harry truly is an ancient Clown
Who has – thankfully – decided to step down.
A total Fraud and Liar, to be sure -
He said several times, "The Border is Secure."

Apparently a wienie, you must understand
He claimed he was badly beaten by a large Rubber Band!
Harry and the Truth have always been miles apart,
And no sane person will really miss the Old Fart.

ER

There are Establishment Republicans
Who think they know what people need;
The problem with that notion is
For a decade their messages voters didn't heed.

Why not? Well, they think they must change
Into a Party most people can't stand!
Sort of a "Leftist Light" they can sell
Believing being "nicer" will make it Grand.

They need to grab their ankles, and pull *hard*
Because playing "nice" against bullies and accusers
Simply makes them so terribly lame that
They continue to be the Designated Losers!

POLLSTERS

To advance any bias or notion, use the Pros
Who claim all control over fears, joys and woes;
No matter what you want people to believe,
They will provide "proof" so you can deceive!

You will have your scholarly words and charts,
(Possibly dreamed up by faculty in Fine Arts);
Of course the Media will profess it is true,
Even from a college or university you never knew.

Some cash to the Profs and more to the "school"
And for a short time this "study" will rule;
So if you want to justify a ruckus or fuss,
Slip the right money to those involved in "Polls R Us"!

16—SUPREME COURT & MEDIA

SUPREME COURT

The Supreme Court was once called "the Nine Old Men;"
Then Ronald Reagan gave them their very first Hen;
The Constitution is what they are supposed to Defend,
But on *that belief,* we no longer can actually Depend!

The pendulum of members politics has often swung Left or Right,
But it rarely has been as poisoned as in the current Fight;
Tradition, Truth, Justice, and what they leave for Later
Have fallen under the oppressive bullying of our Arrogant Dictator!

Our laws now mean *nothing*, based on what they Ruled,
And anyone who still *believes* in them, really is Fooled;
Of the Nine, today we can only honor Three -
The other six must *now* sit down to Pee!

TV MEDIA

The Talking Point presenters of the national "news"
Are really just performers out to sell biased views;
They research *nothing*, and sit around waiting
To be handed whatever is to make today's rating.

To each and every one of them, it must be shipped
Because every single day they all read the exact same script.
Manipulation, propaganda, brainwashing – they have it down flat -
Real, honest Journalism – nothing they *do* even closely is *that*!

The King

The goal each day is always the same:
Defend the Left, make their critics feel shame.
Honesty is not a policy they ever embrace,
All opposition is what they seek to erase.

There was a time when Cronkite was "America's Most Trusted,"
But these brazen turkeys refuse to apologize when their lies are busted.
It is amazing the utterances of the addicts, vultures, weasels and shoats
Somehow don't tangle up and get badly jammed in their throats!

They seem to think if they use the right smile and eye glint
All of our brains will vanish, entirely replaced by lint.
Well, our own futures, tens of millions refuse to botch,
Which is exactly why all these Frauds we don't watch.

17—MORE ENTRIES

OTHER

There are some Opposition Leaders,
At least that's what they are called.
But in fight after fight for many years
They have consistently been badly mauled.

Perhaps they are afraid to offend anyone,
So they sit back and don't even try to scare 'em;
Yet in the end that simply makes them look
Like a group of eunuchs guarding an empty Harem!

POISON IVY LEAGUE

As Evolution began affecting all Creatures,
It altered beliefs and minds, as well as Features.
It grabbed at both Lads and Lasses
Making myriads of each demented asses,
Many of which became Poison Ivy League Teachers!

JEB

Jeb comes from a famous family, "knows" what we want and for that he
    will Push;
He's too dense to realize what we want most is NOT ANOTHER BUSH!

BERNIE

Untruthful Bernie is a life-long Marxist loon;
He truly is a blatant, blabbering old Commie -
He won't admit it (they never do) but he thinks Government
Should really behave like everyone's doting Mommy.

It cannot work, it never has, it always fails badly.
Look, even those who created it collapsed because they went Broke!
If those who tried longest and hardest finally gave up,
Believing Bernie can pull it off is just a twisted Joke!

CNN

The Bobbleheads of CNN – the
Controllist Nattering Nags of the air;
They use fraud every day, in every way
Then repeat it by bragging they *believe* they are Fair.

They have always had slanted views to sell to the Public;
But if you remove the Leftist Lackeys and brainwashed goats,
Those remaining are about 85 poor souls
Too infirm to change their remotes.

They remain daily to spread Lies and Abuse,
Claiming they are True Believers spreading their Word;
Truly, they just do the bidding of a multi-billionaire Bully,
Notorious and infamous Control-freak, Ted the Turd.

17—BETTER LEADERS

In the history of this ailing country
We've had leaders of about every kind;
Both highly and barely educated,
Some brilliant, others slower of mind.

Some were good for our common improvement,
Others seemed lost, lacking or just a Klutz;
But all four of the most recent should never
Have been called POTUS, just referred to as Putz!

We need to choose better people,
Ones who will care about *us* each day;
Reject those who are Sell-outs or Lap dogs,
And together, let us rebuild this USA.